MW01641148

FALSE START-RACE TO PRISON

"My Mom Set Me Up"

DR. ROBIN J. BELL

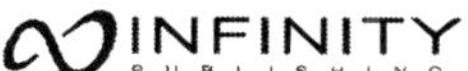

ISBN 978-1-4958-1159-3

Published August 2016

INFINITY PUBLISHING
1094 New DeHaven Street, Suite 100
West Conshohocken, PA 19428-2713
Toll-free (877) BUY BOOK
Local Phone (610) 941-9999
Fax (610) 941-9959
Info@buybooksontheweb.com
www.buybooksontheweb.com

ACKNOWLEDGEMENTS

There are a number of people and without them this book would not be possible, but before I thank them, I want to give thanks to God Almighty. I would like to thank my daughter-in-law, Kimberly, who was a sounding board throughout this journey. I would like to thank my son, Keon, who inspired me to write this book. He may never understand that it was his influence that encouraged me to complete this journey; because of him I can face any challenge. To all of the participants who allowed me to interview them. I am grateful for the amazing and intimate experiences that you each shared with me in order for me to complete this book. Your life experiences have forever changed my life's path; thank you.

Last, but definitely not least, I would like to thank my husband Terry, for being there with me every step of the way. He encouraged me to keep fighting until this journey was over. He invigorated me to continue to write even when life got in the way. He made a conscious effort to learn about this population, because he did not understand their experiences. He assisted significantly in writing this book. He is now and will always be my greatest enthusiast.

MY STORY

The last five years of my military career I served as an Equal Opportunity Advisor for one of the largest organizations in the Department of Defense (DoD). My job was to travel the world and facilitate classes on "Treating Others with Dignity and Respect". That position opened up countless opportunities for me. The world-wide travels shed light on how even in the 21st century there was still incalculable injustice in the world, especially for people of color. While still in the military, I was afforded the opportunity to attend the Atlanta Justice Center for mediation training. Upon completion I became a certified mediator. When I was not using my mediation and facilitation skills traveling the world, I volunteered my time at the Washington DC Superior Court as a Mediator. While mediating, I witnessed countless young black men come through those courtroom doors.

The majority were there for minor drug related or other misdemeanor offenses. I remember such a feeling of sadness seeing those young black men facing the judge. I wondered if they realized the cycle they had begun. Usually they were accompanied by their mothers, grandmothers, court appointed attorneys and sometimes alone. On the other hand, generally when young white men would appear before the judge, they were largely accompanied by their fathers, both parents and/or a paid attorney. While sitting in that courtroom hearing case after case and seeing young black man after young black man have their lives changed forever was a gut wrenching feeling. I knew I wanted to make a difference in the lives of those young men, I just didn't know how I could be impactful.

After retiring from the military in 2005, I decided to go back to school to attain a degree in Counseling Psychology. With a counseling degree I knew I would be able to make a difference in the lives of people who abused drugs. A considerable number of the young men who came through the court system seemed to have minor drug charges. I surmised if they were educated on drug abuse, they may make better life choices. It all seemed like a great plan that could contribute to saving the lives of many "At Risk" African American men. I was in for a huge revelation, really not understanding how convoluted the problem actually was.

For five years I researched African American men with drug addictions who recidivated. There was such a plethora of information that at times it was overwhelming. I could not wrap my head around the statistics about the effects that illegal drugs had on the African American community, they were astonishing. Finally deciding to put pen to paper and stop researching, I devised a dissertation titled: "Shared Experiences of Non-Violent African American Males with Addictions Who Recidivate". I decided to go back to that small, southern, unpromising Virginia town where I had grown up to do my interviews. From my infrequent visits back home, I was not sure if I would have difficulty locating participants to tell their stories.

There was a lot of thought put into what I want this book to convey to the public. First and foremost, I want people to recognize there are entirely too many non-violent, young black boys and men with drug abuse issues locked behind prison walls. Countless numbers are incarcerated because of non-violent, drug related crimes. My argument is not that they shouldn't be punished for the crimes committed, but the time should be appropriate for the crime. I strongly believe if there were more rehabilitation centers and ways to reform this population, the entire world would be a more desirable place for everyone to live.

I was filled with anxiety while making the 4.5hour drive home. I knew there were a lot of guys there who fit the category, but the question was: would they participate? I was apprehensive if anyone would welcome my request. You have to understand where I came from; everyone is not happy if you are what society deems as successful. The young men whom I needed to interview would not know me personally, but may know my parents, siblings or son. I had spoken with one young man there and he said he would be a participant, but was not sure if he could get anyone else to participate.

Once I arrived, I drove around to see who was standing on the street corners. The town only has one red light; therefore, I knew that it would not take long for the word to travel that I was in town and what my mission was. My mom's house was the first stop. I explained to her why I was there. I had not mentioned to her that I was coming home. I just woke up one beautiful May morning and knew it was time to make it happen. When I told her, she commented that "I should be able to accomplish that with no problem". She stated there were a bunch of men on drugs who had nothing better to do than talk to me. You have to understand my mom; she has the biggest heart in the world when it comes to derelicts. Her famous words are "they are somebody's child"

On my way to the hotel where I would be holding the interviews, I stopped by my ex-sister-in-law's house. I am always glad to see her. Of course she asked what brought me in town. I explained to her my reason for being there. She was very excited for me and told me she would put the word out. I informed her where I would be holding the interviews. I stated to her to let whomever was interested know that I would pay for their gas to the hotel and whatever meal they missed during the interviews.

I left her feeling a bit optimistic about the situation. I now had hope that I could get something accomplished before I headed back to Maryland the next day. If anyone could influence the population that I needed, she could. While checking in at the only hotel in town, the receptionist also asked what brought me in town. I explained to her why I was there and she was quite engrossed. She allowed me to reserve a conference room for the interviews.

She began to tell me the difficulties her grandson was having because of drug use. Neither she nor her grandson were African American. She wanted to know if I would be willing to speak with him before I left town and I told her absolutely. I was actually astonished by how enthusiastic the people whom I had shared my reason for the visit were. They were all optimistic of someone attempting to making a difference in the lives of these young black men. You would have thought from their reactions that I came to open up a drug rehabilitation center. It gave me a sense of gratification to know that others were delighted that I was there. They all recognized the need to help the young black men in that town.

I had just gotten to my room and was unpacking my bags when I received a call from the front desk. The receptionist informed me there was a young man there to see me. I was elated to receive that phone call. I hung up, anxious to meet my first participant. I didn't even wait for the elevator; I ran down the stairs. I was in such hurry to begin this process that I failed to take my recorder, briefcase or anything needed to do an interview. All of this was beginning to feel real, it was truly happening.

I could not believe that I actually had someone to interview. Much to my surprise, when I reached the front desk there were three young men waiting to see me. There was no more researching and wondering how all of this would play out, it was all materializing. I was ready to do what I had been preparing to do for so many years. I was about to hear the shared experience of Non-Violent African American Men with Addictions Who Recidivate. It was game time and the ball was in my court.

I composedly introduced myself to the young men whom were waiting right by the elevator and they did the same. To my surprise the young man with whom I had spoken with over the phone weeks ago was standing there with this huge smile on his face. We moved into the interview room where I explained to them my purpose for being there. I informed them of what I was hoping to accomplish. I communicated my passion to be able to make a difference in the lives of men like themselves. One by one they began to tell me how they knew my mom, brother, sister or son. I actually knew all of their parents, but I did not mention it. I felt a sense of relief because of their level of comfort with me.

After we all took a seat, I explained the process. I informed them I would do the interviews individually since it was such a delicate subject. Surprisingly they all wanted to sit in on each other's interviews. They said they had nothing to hide and they already knew everything there was to know about each other. I was OK with that as long as they were comfortable with it. I went over the interview process and passed out the consent forms. I did not assume anything; therefore, I read the consent form aloud. They all acknowledged they understood and each participant signed his individual form. Because of this population it was imperative they understood they were free to discuss any legal issues they may be facing, but to ensure they did not incriminate themselves.

I revealed to them how so many of my friends, classmates and some family members had fallen victim to the "crack epidemic" and how it had forever impacted their lives. I was very cautious because I realized that at least one participant's mother was affected by the "crack epidemic" and was still addicted to drugs. You must remember this is a very small town and not much had changed in nearly 30 years. I stated some facts about recidivism, which means "I fall". I explained it occurs when a person continuously engages in destructive behavior after they have experienced negative consequences from the same or similar behavior.

I informed the participants, that much of the prison population in the United States had grown significantly in the past twenty years. One of the reasons for the growth is the crackdown on illicit drugs, which has created the *"lock them up and throw away the key"* mentality. When inmates such as themselves with a drug addiction go to jail or prison for committing a non- violent crime, they usually do not receive drug treatment while incarcerated. After being released they still have the same craving for drugs, which in most instances leads them back to the life they were living before being incarcerated.

I expressed to the participants that if more non-violent criminals with an addiction had accessibility to drug rehabilitations centers, there is a very strong possibility that the recidivism rate would be lower. It was important they understood that according to recent studies about 80% of prisoners have a drug problem. Usually black males, just like themselves, between the ages of 25-29 are the leading racial group incarcerated in the United States. I informed the participants that more black men were incarcerated today, than were enslaved in1850, after the Civil War. I will never forget the looks on their faces when they heard that statement. When this population is incarcerated it not only affects them, but the entire African American race is impacted. I wanted them to understand that where they live also has an impact on their recidivism rate. Most offenders, such as the participants live in neighborhoods where the crime rate is high and the income is low.

It was a wonderful experience to have the trust of the participants. After the interviews with the initial three, it only got better. By the end of the day, I had interviewed six participants. That following morning I had five more young men waiting to do interviews. I was thrilled at the trust those gentlemen bestowed in me. Everyone was brutally honest and appreciated that I cared enough to listen to their stories.

I headed back to Maryland later that evening feeling absolutely elated. I was so inspired by their brutal honesty and heart wrenching stories. I knew this was just the beginning to something much greater. There was considerable work to be done. I was determined to be a leading force for this population of young black men. In the next few days, I interviewed five more participants back in Maryland. Their stories were just as incredible as the men in Virginia. All of the participants had the same plight, but every one of them had an unusual and heart wrenching story to tell.

The Participant's Textual and Structural Description

The detailed and expressive narratives from the participants' interviews generated the depth needed to illustrate each of their lived experiences. The experience of being an African American male with an addiction who had recidivated was portrayed in each participant's description. The first participant whose name will be Scott for the purpose of his privacy was a 24-year-old African American male who is the product of a two-parent household. Scott has been arrested five times and incarcerated three times. He was 17 years old at the time of his first arrest. He did not graduate from high school, and his drug of choice is marijuana. Scott is not married and does not have any children. Before the interview began, he appeared very passionate about telling his story. His body language showed that he was comfortable as well as confident. Scott begun by telling me about his childhood.

Textual description of Scott's experience in his words

> I was raised in a very loving home. I can remember my parents encouraging me to stay active in sports and not to hang with the wrong crowd and to get my education. It was very important to my parents that I had a respectful upbringing. I didn't listen and did what I wanted to do, I was hardheaded. I started getting high at 13. I am ashamed to tell you the first place that I ever got high; it was in the back of an abandoned church. The first time I got high, I enjoyed it and kept doing it. I knew right from wrong, but I got with the wrong crowd. I remember hanging out with my friends getting high and watching a few of them selling weed. The ones that were selling

was wearing the newest sneakers and the flyest clothes. I wanted to have the latest sneaker without having to ask my parents to buy them so I started selling weed.

Summation of Scott's experience

Additionally, he started selling drugs at age 14, and he sold drugs for almost a year before he was arrested for possession of marijuana. The first time he was arrested, he did not receive any jail time. He stopped selling for a little while, but before long he felt as though the heat was off of him and he returned to selling. Eventually he was arrested for selling drugs again when he was sixteen and was sent to a juvenile detention center for six months. He was 17 years old when he was apprehended with a very large amount of drugs and was sent to a state prison for two years. According to Scott, his first prison experience was nothing like he expected; he admitted that prison was really scary. He continued to reiterate that prison was a horrible place, and he tries to inform other young males that prison is not a place they want to go. He encourages all of them, especially the young ones, to stay on the right track and not to get in legal trouble.

While in prison, Scott took mandatory drug classes and was enrolled in a drug program. During his incarceration he had a lot of support from his family and had visitors each week. His mother and father would both visit on Sundays along with other family members. Upon his release from prison, he moved back home with his parents. Scott was placed on probation after being released and had to report to his probation officer once a week. He had a good relationship with his probation officer and was not cited for any probation violations. Approximately three to four months after being released, Scott found employment with a temporary employment agency. He was placed in a bank inputting data entry for the taxation department. The job only lasted about six months. He is now unemployed, but he is seeking employment, and has not used drugs for almost a year. He would like to work with rappers and mix music to make a living.

Scott did receive drug treatment while incarcerated and he felt as though it was very helpful. He learned a lot about how drugs negatively affect him and the longer he used the more likely it was that he would go back to prison. The classes also made him realize that drugs take a toll on the body as well as the mind. He has been drug free for almost a year and attributes that largely to the education he received during drug treatment while incarcerated.

I asked Scott how he felt about the number of black men locked up and how it impacted the entire African American race. His first remark was how it was hard to get a job after being locked up. As a black man with a felony he stated that he was embarrassed to write on his job application that he had been to prison. He stated that it was humiliating to disclose that information to white people. He feels that white people already look down on blacks and to be a black man with a criminal record only makes it worse. Scott understood that he was one of the few who had gotten locked up for drugs and got a second chance in life, especially from his town. He said that he would take full advantage of the opportunity and never go back to prison because it was a very humiliating experience.

The last question was; did he feel that social disorganization played a role in his decision to become involved with drugs? Social Disorganization is how a neighborhood's composition can influence an individual's behavior. Does living in the inner city, small drug infested towns, lack of employment, race, and unstable homes play a major role in recidivism? Scott expressed that the lack of employment was one of the reasons he felt as though he had to sell drugs in order to make money. He said that unless you were white or acted white your chances of getting a good job was very slim. Scott described the city as a small hick town without a lot of opportunities for blacks.

He considered his family as a good loving family, but not much to offer him in the way of finances. He was glad to be raised by both parents because most of his friends did not have their fathers in the home. He felt that if his father was not in the home that he would be in more trouble than he already was. His parents instilled great values in him and his siblings, but they both worked hard in order to put food on the table. Scott expressed that nothing came easy in that small hick town and as soon as he made it big in the rap world, he was out of there!

Donovan's textual description of his experience

The second participant is a 31-year-old African American male who is the product of a single parent household. Donovan has been arrested three times and incarcerated twice. He was 26 years old at the time of his first arrest. He received his GED while incarcerated, and his drug of choice is marijuana. He is not married, but he has two children. Donovan displayed a willingness to talk and appeared very comfortable during the interview.

> My childhood was fairly decent, I mean I never had problems growing up; I got pretty much what I wanted as far as sneakers and stuff. I lived with my mom pretty much all my life; my dad got locked up for murder when I was small. I never knew my father until recently because he was incarcerated most of his life. He got out for a short period, but is now back in. By the time he got out of prison the first time I was grown and we kind of built a relationship

because when I was small I never really knew him. I never visited him while in prison, he used to call me and write and stuff, but I never really wanted to talk to him because I mean, I never knew him. I didn't really care too much for him, but then after he got out and then I talked to him, I got to know him, we built a relationship. I mean, now he's cool with me. The first time I got high I was 12 and it was not a good experience and it wasn't peer pressure.

Donovan's structural description of his experience

Donovan shared that he was not influenced by his friends at a young age to use drugs. He revealed that the first time he tried drugs he felt quite ridiculous. He admitted that after trying drugs a few times, he began to like the effects, which ultimately fueled his frequent drug use. He stated that he has used cocaine in the past, but marijuana is his drug of choice and he also enjoys drinking. Donovan stated that he is slowly declining his drug use because he no longer gets the same effect from it that he once did. He was last incarcerated approximately two years ago in a county jail. While incarcerated, he was offered drug and alcohol classes, but refused them because he felt as though he could rehabilitate himself. During his time in jail he received a lot of support from his family. His daughter was born while he was incarcerated.

She would come with his girlfriend to visit, but was too young to understand the experience.

Donovan's textual description of his experience

> Well I moved in with my girlfriend because we were still together after I got out. She pretty much... She had helped me get everything back situated. Then it wasn't too long after that though, we split up. But my time in jail made me a whole lot smarter, because I was like, for real, before I went to jail that's when I had been doing cocaine or whatever. Then when I was locked up, like I said, I didn't think people really need rehabilitation. I feel like it's all in your head. That time that I was locked up, I did a whole lot of thinking, you know what I'm saying? I felt that was something I never needed. That was another thing I was just doing because people around me was doing it.

Donovan's structural description

After being released from his last incarceration Donovan never did cocaine again. He realized that getting high was only hindering him from doing anything positive in life. Being incarcerated gave him an opportunity to do a lot of soul-searching. He admits that he does drink every day and may very well have a drinking problem. Donovan had a job before he was incarcerated but lost it while in jail. He was approved for work release by the jail, but the judge denied the request; therefore, he did not have a job waiting after being released from jail. He is still unemployed and still drinks every day, but does not think he needs to participate in the Alcoholic Anonymous program. He said that he felt rehabilitated after doing this interview because he felt as though all he needed was someone who cared and someone to listen.

I asked Donovan if he felt that drug rehabilitation while incarcerated would help people who are addicted to drugs. He felt that it would if they could not kick the habit themselves. Even though he felt strongly about people being able to quit doing drugs if they want to, it was a little different with alcohol. Donovan drank every day and realized it hindered him from getting a job and being a productive citizen, but he said he cannot function unless he has his drink first thing. I asked Donovan if Alcohol Anonymous was offered to him today would he accept and he stated, yes he would.

Donovan expressed that in this particular town, no one cared, especially white people. He stated that he was still angry over the fact the judge would not allow him work release while incarcerated. He said he was not a danger to society and he would be able to help support his child. He figured the judge would rather see black folks down and out than trying to help themselves. He said he knew plenty of white boys locked up with him that were able to do work release. Donovan expressed that he could not wait to get his life together so that he would be able offer a better life for his children.

I asked him if he realized the negative impact that mass incarceration of black men had on their children. He said there wasn't a day that went by that he didn't ask God not to let him be like his father. Donovan felt that his father's incarceration had a considerable impact on the way he turned out. He said it was not that big of a deal back then because the majority of his friends didn't have fathers in the home. He knew it was a void, but did not realize until he was older the real impact it had on his life being raised in a single parent home. He feels as though his mother would not have had the struggle that she encountered if his father had been in the home. Donovan said he was told his entire life that his father was not a bad person, but made a horrible mistake because he was on drugs. Donovan suggested that his father's choice to use drugs had completely destroyed his life and Donovan would never allow that to happen to him.

I asked Donovan what could he do to get his life on track? He stated that having a job would be a start, but because he is a felon, the minute anyone, mainly white people see his application, it's over. He does not want to work the rest of his life doing laborious work. He would like to have a good job paying good money. At this point he feels that there is no future for him unless he moves out of his small town. He realizes that he has a lot of work to do on his end in order to possibly get a decent paying job anyplace. He realizes he has to stay out of trouble with the law. He said in order to do that, he may have to let go of some of his friends who influences him to do things that he would not otherwise do.

The last question that I asked Donovan was how he felt about his mother making the choice to have him without being married to his father. He said that his mother was a wonderful mom and did the best she could and it was not her fault that his dad was sorry. He said that it is common in the black culture for women to have babies out of wedlock. He said all of his mom's friends had babies and no husbands. He said mainly white folk in that town get married before they have kids. He said he realizes that's the right thing to do, but he's OK and so is his daughter. His mom did the best she could and he loves her no matter what.

Nathan's textual description of his experience

The third participant is a 26-year-old African American male who was also raised in a single parent home. He has been arrested three times and incarcerated twice. He was 18 years old at the time of his first arrest. Nathan did not graduate from high school. His drug of choice is marijuana. He is not married, but has one child. He appeared to be nervous before the interview. Once the interview began, he became more relaxed. The interview began with Nathan describing his behavior problems in childhood.

> My childhood was alright. I never had to ask for much, my mother and father provided me with pretty much everything I needed. I was a problem child and was constantly in trouble at school. At one point I lived with both my parents, but they were never married. I lived with my father at one point because of me acting up in school. I spent most of my childhood with my mama. I was 15 years old the first time I used drugs. I started doing drugs because everyone around me was using and by adults telling me to stay away from certain people and drugs, only made me want to do it more. The first time I did drugs it was a good experience.

Nathan's structural description of his experience

Nathan was last arrested and incarcerated because he failed a mandatory urinalysis while on probation. He revealed that he believes in drug rehabilitation, but was never offered any classes during the times he spent incarcerated. After he was released from jail his last incarceration, he was put on probation. While on probation he was instructed to take mandatory urinalysis; he passed them all and is no longer on probation. Nathan revealed that he thinks he needs drug and alcohol rehabilitation, but has never really known who to talk to in order to begin the process. He did not have a job after he was released from jail and still does not have employment, but is actively searching. Nathan moved home to live with his mother upon release, and he currently still resides there.

Nathan feels as though there is not much hope for him in this small town. He spoke of how there are no organized sports for black people unless you play football or basketball in school. There is nowhere to go and nothing to do. He really appreciated me coming from up north to even listen to them because no one there cares. He wished his mom had moved up north after she had him, then he would have something to do. His father has people in D.C. and he would love to move up there. The only thing stopping him now is his child. He does not want his child to be without her father.

Even though his parents co-parented most of his life, he wished his parents had lived together all the time. He preferred living with his mom because she wasn't as strict, but his dad was very strict. He realizes that he took advantage of his mom and gave her a hard time. He said if he had it to do all over again, he would have been an obedient son. He now understands the agony his mom must have gone through trying to raise a disobedient young black boy who was determined to do what he wanted to do. He recognizes that being rebellious has gotten him to where he is in life right now. That being broke, jobless, a felon and addicted to drugs. He is afraid that he will start back using because there is not much else to do in this town. He does want his child to have a better life than he does but right now, it does not look good.

He resents ever putting himself in a position to make the bad choices that has caused him to be incarcerated three times. Nathan vows that he is not going back to jail, it was such a demeaning place. Having to ask permission to do everything, like a slave. I asked Nathan if he felt like prison was a new form of slavery for black men and he said absolutely. Nathan said that mostly everyone in charge was white. I asked him what could blacks do to change the vicious cycle. He said stop getting in trouble! My last question to Nathan was-does your mother hold any responsibility for your demise? He looked at me quizzically and said no-*he* made the bad choices and there was nothing his mother could have done to prevent that.

Jonah's textual description of his experience

The fourth participant is a 30-year-old African American male who was raised by his grandmother. Jonah has been arrested six times and incarcerated five. He was 22 years old at the time of his first arrest. He did not graduate from high school, and his drug of choice is marijuana. Jonah is not married, but has two children. He seemed eager to share his experience as an African American male with an addiction and who has recidivated. The interview commenced as he discussed his mother's abandonment of him and his gratitude for his grandmother who raised him.

> I didn't live with either of my parents. I never knew my dad and my mother, she was in and out. But like I said, I was raised by my grandmother. My childhood was average. I did a lot more than a lot of my friends. I had been overseas. I had every pair of Jordan's that came out. But then on the flip side I was around a lot of drugs at a young age, seeing a lot of bad things. My mother has been on drugs almost my whole life and was never really there for me. For the record, I was raised by my grandmother. Thank God for my grandmother. That was a blessing.

Jonah's first experience with drug use was when he was 11 years old. He said that he did it to impress older girls because that was what his friends were doing. He continued to do drugs, and ultimately because of his drug use he started committing crimes. When he was 22 years old, he was convicted of writing bad checks and sent to jail. He explained that his first experience was very frightening.

> My first experience, all I remember was, this is not for me, it's not for me. You are in a room and you can't leave. You can't watch TV when you want. You got to use the bathroom beside somebody. I mean, it was horrible, but the more you get into it, you get used to it because you already know what to expect. But the hardest thing for me was that I couldn't even leave when I wanted to. I had to stay right here. There's no way you're leaving out. It took a long time for me to get that through my head. When they closed the door, I tried to call them back; I go "hey can I make a phone call? Can I have a piece of papers? Can I have a magazine or book? Can you just come and talk to me? Can I have some Neosporin? As soon as it opens, you just want to step outside of it and just sit there. I had a lot of support while incarcerated and had visits from my girlfriend and mother weekly. I did not let my girlfriend bring my kids to visit; it was too much for me to handle.

Upon release from jail Jonah moved in with his girlfriend, but that living arrangement was short lived.

> When I got out I didn't have a job, but a few months later, I found a guy that was cutting grass, so I walked up to him and asked him. Now I do landscaping by myself. When I first got out it was hard, because I had to ask her

> for a lot because like I said for the first couple of months, I didn't have a job. My family really looked out for me a lot, but then when I got back on my feet a little bit, I moved back out of my girlfriend's house. I paid my debts off, but then landscaping is only seasonal. After that, it's like man.... I got a felony too, so there's not too many jobs going to hire you, so I had to go back to square one, fast food for a while.

Jonah was on probation upon his release from jail and had a good relationship with his probation officer. He was not offered any form of drug or alcohol rehabilitation while incarcerated, but was subjected to mandatory urinalysis. He stated that his probation officer was lenient and worked with him to keep him from going back to prison. He admitted to failing several urinalysis test, but was not reported for violating his probation. After failing the second urinalysis, he was put on color code, which means he was monitored more closely via telephone and was given urinalysis more frequently. Jonah realized that the color code was forcing him to stop using marijuana because he did not want to go back to jail. He was mandated to take drug classes after two failed urinalyses, which he did attend. He is still on probation and has passed his last 2-urinalysis test. Jonah stated that his addiction and lack of education makes it hard for him to get a good job, which would allow him to provide for his children.

Jonah is currently living with his grandmother along with his mother who is on drugs and another of his grandmother's adult addicted children. The living situation is not good because it appears as though none of the adults want to get their lives together. He is particularly disappointed in his mother who has been addicted to drugs his entire life. Jonah says that it is embarrassing to see his mother in the streets high or hustling for drugs. He tries not to hang in the same circles as his mom. Because the town is so small it is almost impossible not to run into her out in the streets on occasion.

Jonah has tried moving to another city to get away from the small town and the embarrassment of his mother, but finds it difficult because he does not have a driver's license. Regardless of where he goes, he still is a felon and the odds of getting a decent paying job is slim. He initially thought that the leniency shown toward him from his probation officer was helping him, but realized it was only setting him up to violate. Jonah understands that even though it is his responsibility to not use drugs, he initially thought he was getting a free pass from his Probation Officer (PO). I asked him if he ever considered that his PO wanted to give him another chance and not send him back to prison.

I explained to him there was a difference between his PO being cool and his PO understanding that relapse was a part of rehabilitation. I asked Jonah if he had any idea of how many black men would be locked up if they were sent back to prison after failing one urinalysis. I explained to him this is where drug rehabilitation would possibly be an effective tool if it was offered to everyone who was locked up with a drug problem. I clarified that drug rehabilitation is not for people who need it, but for people who want it. If he or anyone else afforded the opportunity only took advantage of it, the experience may change their lives.

Jonah said that he would be willing to go into drug rehabilitation because he did not want his children to grow up exposed to drugs, like he was at such an early age. Jonah thinks that it was inevitable that he turned out the way he did. He said there were really no positive role models in his life-especially his family. He said he use to dream about having a normal family who sat down to dinner together and had rules for their children. He praises his grandmother because without her, he realizes that his life would have been pure hell because of his mother's addiction and her inability to care for him.

Lamont's textual description of his experience

Lamont is a 25-year-old African American male who is the product of a two-parent household. He has been arrested four times and incarcerated twice. He received his GED while incarcerated. He is not married, he has no children, and his drug of choice is marijuana. He was very enthusiastic to tell his story and did not waste any time when the interview began. The interview began with him describing his early exposure with the adults in his life using drugs.

> I didn't have a bad childhood, I mean my momma never worked, she stayed home with us, but my daddy's been working all my life. I mean, from the time I can remember, my daddy's been working. I always got what I wanted, but still they was the type like, you know they made sure we were taken care of, but anything extra went to them having their lil fun, you know? They had a little addiction too when I was growing up, so all the extra went to their habit. But the necessities, we had necessities, just not the, you know what I mean? The first time I used drugs, I was 14. I made the decision to use because of my friends. Everybody, I mean, I had this older dude, he was about 21, he'd been a friend of the family for a long time. And he had me in the room with him, we was in there playing a game and he rolled up and was like, "Have you ever tried this?" I was like, "no." He was like "Why don't you try it, see how you like it?" And I tried it, and turned out I liked it pretty good. I did, I liked it pretty good.
>
> I got my GED while I was in jail. I got my GED in jail, and I was also ...we had like this church. We had a church in jail, like this black minister

would come to church every Sunday, and I started like this, almost like a little makeshift choir in jail. See, that's what I do, I sing, but in jail, I made like a little makeshift choir, me and a couple of dudes, and every Sunday, we use to get up there, like real church, tried to make it feel a little bit more like home. That's another thing I did while in jail. It didn't cut back on my time, but brought more people to church.

Lamont's structural description of his experience

Lamont stated that prison was the worst experience that he has ever had and that he never wants to go back. He was involved in an incident in jail that caused him to be sent to the hole for two weeks, and after the experience of being locked up in a cell that was only large enough to spread his arms, no windows, a bright light shining all night, a commode at the head of a mattress that was on the floor and not having anyone to talk to, made him realize that was no way for any human to live. He vowed that situation changed his life forever, and he knew that after surviving such an ordeal, he would never go back to jail. Before his release, Lamont married his girlfriend whom he had been dating for a few years while he was incarcerated.

Once he was released, he moved back home with his parents. He has not been with his wife since his release and will file for a divorce in the very near future. Since his release, Lamont has not attended any drug classes. He stated that he really appreciated the fact that I cared enough about the people in that county to come out and hear their story. He spoke about the lack of opportunities in the small town and how young people have nothing to do to keep them occupied. Far too many of the black males have felonies and or an addiction, which hinder them from earning a decent living.

He thanked me "for coming all the way from up North to talk with [him], because no one in his town cares." He admitted that if he was afforded the opportunity to attend drug rehabilitation, he would. He stated that he had asked his probation officer about attending weekend drug rehabilitation classes, but there are none offered in the vicinity on the weekends, which is the only time that he could attend because of his job. He felt as though he had to choose work over going to drug rehabilitation. Without a job, he would be returned to prison because maintaining employment is one of the stipulations of his probation. He hopes that in the near future he will be able to attend drug rehabilitation classes as well as maintain his job.

I asked Lamont if he thought his parent's addiction contributed to his use of drugs at such an early age. He thinks that it may have had something to do with it. He knew his parents did drugs but never really thought about it as a child. No one ever said anything negative about his parents' drug use so as a kid he thought it was a way of life. Because his parents provided food, shelter and clothes, he never really thought much about it as a kid. Lamont had friends whose parents did not use drugs and some of those friends still didn't live as well as he did.

He remembers going with friends home and they had no lights, because their parents could not pay the bill. He had friends who would eat at his house because they didn't have food at home. Lamont never held his parents' addiction against them and never used it as an excuse for his short comings in life. He does now resent the adult who introduced him to drugs at such a young age. He knows that his life would be totally different if he had never been introduced to drugs.

Lamont was incarcerated for selling drugs. His rationale for selling was because as a young black man in this town, he would never be able to find a decent job. At that time, he did not realize that if he finished school, stayed out of trouble that his possibilities of getting a job would have been better. He looked at the other young men there that has finished school, stayed out of trouble and still had nothing to show for it. Lamont wanted nice things and he wanted them his way. He admits that once he started selling that he got really good at it and was respected by the younger boys in the town.

He said the money was fast and he never thought about stopping until he got caught. Even though he has been arrested four times, the first three only slowed him down, but did not deter him from selling. His first incarceration was a short stint and even that did not deter him. Once he was released he started right back. Now he really felt the need because he had a criminal record and possibly could not find other employment.

After his last stint in prison, Lamont said he finally gets it. As mentioned above, the two weeks in the hole was a significant emotional event that changed his life. Lamont said that it was the grace of God that he is still sane. He said it was the most horrifying and demeaning experience of his life. He expressed that no man should ever be treated like that unless he had violently murdered someone. Lamont said he does not understand how people survive in the hole. If nothing else changed his life, that experience did.

He shared the experience of having a girlfriend while in prison and relying on her to be there for him. He said that he could not have made it through without her support and knowing he would have someone there for him when he returned home. He didn't too much worry about her being unfaithful because she lived with his parents and came to visit every week. While he was dealing he provided her with everything she needed and most of what she wanted. He decided while he was incarcerated that it would be a great idea to get married, but his parents were against it. They encouraged him to wait until he was released, but he did not want to wait and his girlfriend accepted his proposal.

They got married about six months before it was time for him to be released and things began to change. After they were married he put her name on his bank account. For a small town black boy, he had a hefty account. Even though it was dirty money, that was the money he used to survive on while in prison. His parents were against him putting her name on the account and he did not understand why, that was his wife. After about a month of being married, his now wife's visits began to get further and further apart. When he would question her, she would come up with one excuse after another.

He also noticed that his mother had stopped mailing his monthly bank statements. Lamont realized that when he would call home before lights out, around 10:00pm, sometimes his wife was not home and his parents didn't know where she was. He said that was one of the worst feelings in the world, to be locked up and thinking that your wife may be cheating on you. He was going crazy and could do absolutely nothing about it. Regardless of how many times he would question his parents or his wife, they all said that everything was fine. He knew in his heart that something wasn't right and being helpless was driving him insane, literally.

The day that Lamont was released, his parents came to pick him up, but no wife. His mother told him as soon as he got in the car, that right after they got married his wife starting seeing someone else. His mother suspects she was already seeing someone, but only wanted to have access to his bank account. Lamont was furious. He was furious with his parents for not telling him and livid with his wife for betraying him. He had done a lot of bad things in his life, but he had never cheated on her. His heart was broken, knowing he had been manipulated.

At that point he did not even want to go home. All this time locked up and waiting for this day and this is what he goes home to. His real reason for not wanting to go home was because he was afraid of what he might do to her when he got there. Prison was almost an unbearable experience and the last thing he wanted was to go back. He knew if he went home that he would regret it, so he asked his parents to take him to his relative's house in a nearby town. He stayed there for a few weeks until he got his head together. He spoke with his soon to be ex-wife on the phone and expressed his resentment for what she did. He told her that he was coming home and it would befit her and all involved to be long gone.

Lamont went home that day and has not to this day seen his wife. It has been two years. He plans on getting a divorce, but does not have the funds. Any monies that he gets doing odd jobs is not enough to get a divorce. He has no desire to ever be with her again. He use to see other inmates get Dear John letters, but he never thought it would happen to him. Not only did he learn that crime doesn't pay, neither does putting all of your trust in a person. He says the only one he puts all of his trust in now is God!

Avayon's textual description of his experience

Avayon is a 30-year-old African American male who is the product of a single parent household. He has been arrested six times and incarcerated six times. He was 22 years old at the time of his first arrest. He is a high school graduate and has four children, but he is not married. He appeared nervous about doing the interview. The interview began with him describing the effect that peer pressure played on his initial drug use. Avayon's first experience with drugs was not at a very early age, unlike the other participants; he first experimented with drugs when he was 19 or 20 years old.

> My mother raised me and my uncle did more for me than my dad ever has. I might have been about five when my dad bought me a pair of shoes and that was it. I know him, but I just speak to him, I see him. I started using drugs because of friends to be honest with you. I drank a little, but as far as smoking weed or cigarettes, I didn't do that until after I graduated high school. One night we were at a party and my friends was like, "Hit this blunt." I hit it and I guess what you call a buzz, it increased

> and it relaxed me so I've been smoking weed ever since. I've been trying to quit. I've slowed myself down myself. I used to smoke trash can bags full of weed because one of my friends was a drug dealer. That's all we did was smoke trash can bags full of weed and play video games. I went from smoking like a trash bag like that to a fruit bowl, to an ounce, to maybe a blunt, to two blunts a month. It wouldn't even be that maybe a half blunt.

Avayon's structural description of his experience

The first time that Avayon was incarcerated, the experience was not as bad as he had imagined it would be. He had seen a lot of movies and expected to see people getting raped and a lot of fights, but was pleasantly surprised throughout the six times he was incarcerated. He was never sent to a prison, but served all of his incarcerations in jails; he has spent over four years of his life incarcerated. Avayon had weekly visits from his mother during each of his incarcerations. He did not allow his children to visit him in jail because he did not want them to think this was an acceptable or desirable way of life.

Upon release, Avayon moved back in with his mother and is currently trying to get a job so that he can move into his own place. He realizes that he is a grown man with four children who needs to be able to support them. Now that he has cut back significantly on his marijuana use, he hopes that he will be able to pass a urinalysis and get a steady paying job. Avayon stated that if he had it to do all over again, he would have never touched marijuana. Being addicted to marijuana has cost him far too many years of freedom, too many years away from his children, and years he can never get back. Avayon stated that he would attend Alcoholic Anonymous if he could find a location that was convenient for him, because he does not have transportation.

He did not want to talk much about his upbringing because he said it was not the most pleasant way for a child to live. As he stated above, his father was not an important part of his life. As far as he is concerned he was just another nigga on the street. He saw how his mother struggled to care for him and his siblings with absolutely no help from the bum. His mother's brother helped the family tremendously. Without his uncle being an influence in his life, he thinks he would probably be in prison right now.

Even though his uncle use to smoke weed, he never did it around him. He was the only male figure he had to look up to. His uncle helped his mom with the bills. Even though there were times when there wasn't enough food, or many presents for Christmas, Avayon always felt loved. He remembers hearing his mom practically begging his dead beat dad to help her out financially. He remembers thinking that when he got older he would be the man of the house so that his mother would not have to struggle so much. Now that he looks back, he realizes that his drug addiction has caused him to miss out on a lot of opportunities in life. His chances of helping his mom or even his own four kids are slim.

Avayon regrets the fact that he ever smoked the first joint. Every time he was incarcerated it was because of his drug use. Whether it was for possession, parole violation or failed urinalysis, the common denominator was weed. He feels that weed has essentially ruined his life and will be his demise if he doesn't get it together soon. He has four children that he needs to support. Avayon's worst nightmare is that his children will feel about him, the way that he feels about his father. He tries to see his children as much as possible, but realizes that he could do better.

I asked Avayon if he felt his mother had any bearing on the way that he turned out as a man. He thought about the question for a while and said, his mom did the best she could with what she had. He said his mother does not bear any of the responsibility for the way his life has turned out. He said his mom always bailed him out when he was in trouble. Avayon said she always managed to get the money from someplace and never missed a week visiting him while incarcerated. He feels that his mom is his rock and without her he would probably still be locked up.

His plan is to find a job, have a relationship with his children and move out of his mom's house. He expressed the difficulties of finding a decent paying job with a felony on his record-actually two felonies. Avayon's major concern is becoming a better father and a better man. Even though the small town has nothing to offer young people, especially black people, he has no desire to move any place else. This is home and all that he knows!

Brad's textual description of his experience

Brad is a 24-year-old African American male who is the product of a two- parent household. He has been arrested eight times and incarcerated six times. Brad did not graduate from high school. His drug of choice is heroin, he is considered married by common law, and he has no children. During the initial introduction and signing of the consent form, he appeared preoccupied. I asked if he was still interested in participating and reminded him that he could back out at any time. He assured me that he definitely wanted to be a part of the interviews. The interview proceeded with Brad telling me about his parents' drug and alcohol use and its influence on his own life.

> As a child I can't say I was really bad. It was a bad childhood. I would see my parents drink and smoke a lot. I guess when I was about eight, me and my brother found my daddy's cocaine

stash. I started drinking and smoking about the age of eight. I don't really know why I didn't say no. I guess it was because of all the peer pressure. I didn't really do any heavy drugs until I was about 15. Around then I started doing cocaine. Soon after that I probably started heroin. I like both the drugs. That was probably about the time I started doing crime. Probably around 17, I was arrested the first time. I don't really have a reason why I did what I did. My mama she was good. She was a real good mama. I don't blame anyone but myself.

Brad's structural description of his experience

Brad began the interview process by describing his first experience with drugs. He stated that it was not a good experience because he hallucinated after smoking marijuana. He admitted that his first experimentation with drugs was because of his brother. He looked up to his brother and wanted to be like him when they were younger; therefore, whatever his brother did, he wanted to do as well. He admits that he no longer has a relationship with his brother; after his first incarceration, they rarely communicated. He explained that his first experience with prison life was much like he expected.

During his first incarceration he had a couple of visits from his mother and a few visits from friends.

During his second and third incarcerations, he rarely, if ever, had visitors. Brad has a common-law wife, but they have not communicated at all since his release. He realizes that his wife deserves a better life than he has provided for her. He stated that each time he goes to prison, he promises himself that it is going to be his last, but with his addiction he is continuously breaking the law in order to get money for drugs.

When Brad was released from prison the last time, he went to live with his parents and he still resides there. He does not have any children; therefore, his only responsibility is to care for himself. He has been released from prison for nearly two months and has not yet secured steady employment. He does odd jobs and knows that his lack of education and felony charges hamper his chances of securing a well-paying job. Brad is not currently on probation and states that he will do everything required of him in order to stay out of prison. He completed several drug rehabilitation classes while incarcerated, but he did not feel as though they were long enough for him to benefit from them. He stated that he would be willing to go to residential drug rehabilitation if he could afford it and if he could still be able to maintain employment.

Brad remembers his mother and father getting high and often fighting over who did the last of the drugs. He knew as a child that was not how normal people lived, but that was all he knew.

He felt that his dad was not a good man or father because he would put his hands on his mother. He remembers times when his parents were fighting that he would hide in the closet and put his hand over his ears to silence the cussing and yelling. He remembers having thoughts of hurting his father for the things he did to his mother. Brad vowed that he would never hit a lady and he never has. Even though he has had some violent arguments with his common-law wife, he has never hit her.

Even though Brad's brother was older, he still would not challenge his father when he was fighting his mom. Brad looked up to his brother because he made him feel safe. His brother comforted him when there was chaos in the house, which was most of the time. There were times when his parents weren't fighting, but then they were so stoned out of their minds, they had no time for him and his brother. His brother ensured he ate and got to school when his mom was either high or coming off of a high.

Brad realizes that as far as society is concerned, he is considered a low life who should be locked away. He hates the way employers look at him when he applies for a job. He admits that he is ashamed of all of the wrong that he has done, but he still has morals. He regrets the fact that he has wasted so much of his life because of his drug use. He does not blame anyone for his bad choices but himself. I asked Brad if he felt that his upbringing had any impact on some of the choices he has made in life? He said it was a bad choice to ever use drugs, but it was his choice. Drugs are the cause of all of his problems.

Throughout the interview, Brad mentioned several times that if could get into a drug rehabilitation center, he would go today! He would like to reconnect with his brother, whom he loves dearly. His brother started out a little shaky in his teenage years, but eventually got his life together. His brother never visited him in prison. He understands if his brother has given up on him because at times he gives up on himself. Now that his parents are older, they don't use drugs anymore. Both his parents are old and tired and have little tolerance for his criminal activity.

Brad wants more than anything in the world to get out of his parents' house, find a good job and be free of drugs. Drugs have ruined his life and before he leaves this world he wants to know how it feels to be drug free, working and happy. He said he cannot ever remember being happy. Brad ended the interview with tears in his eyes and asked if there was anything that I could do to help?

Carlton's textual description of his experience

Carlton is a 26-year-old African American male who is the product of a two-parent household. He has been arrested ten times and incarcerated three times. He was 16 years old at the time of his first arrest. He is married with two children, and his drug of choice is cocaine. Carlton appeared enthusiastic about telling his lived experience and actually began sharing his story before the recording begin.

> I was born in Phoenix, but raised most of my life in Dallas, Texas before I moved here. I did have good parents, brothers and sisters. They always gave me what I wanted, but in my teenage years I became more interested in females and da street than sports and family life. I started hanging with the wrong crowd and making bad decisions. I started on a path that led me to drugs. Drugs has been a big part of my life for too many years and I wanna live a normal life. I wanna wake up and not even think about drugs. I lived with both my parents and my dad tried to be a good influence; he was always around, he was a great mentor, but I was hardheaded and determined to do what I wanted to do. I broke every rule and every curfew that my parents ever set.

Carlton's structural description of his experience

Carlton's first experiences with drugs occurred in the company of his friends. His friends were introduced to drugs before him; therefore, he wanted to be cool and accepted, so it was not long before he conformed. He expressed that while he was high, he felt a sense of confidence that he had never felt before. He felt that being high made it easier for him to approach girls, which was very important to him. His first drug experience was with marijuana, which was eventually the gateway to harder drugs. He revealed that because of his drug use, he committed numerous crimes that he would not have otherwise committed. He expressed that it has been a struggle trying to remain drug-free and to live a life that is acceptable to society.

During Carlton's last incarceration he had a lot of moral support from his family, but not a lot of financial support. After he was released from prison the second time, he spent most of his days getting high instead of looking for a job. He moved back in with his wife and had great intentions of getting a job and providing for his family, but with a felony it was very difficult for him to obtain employment. Carlton stated that he has never been offered any employment or drug rehabilitation assistance upon being released from prison. He admitted that he never inquired about rehabilitation, but if afforded the opportunity he would have accepted it.

The last time he was sent back to prison was due to violating his parole by failing a mandatory urinalysis test. He is no longer on parole and is currently separated from his wife. He states that he has no reservations about his wife distancing herself from him until he is drug-free. Unfortunately, because of his addiction, his family is not able to live the life they deserve. His wife works, but her income is not sufficient to care for her and their two children. Therefore, other family members constantly pick up the slack in order for his wife and children to have food on the table and a roof over their heads. Carlton understands the stress on his wife and children and hopes to someday soon be able to support his family the way he believes a man should. His ultimate goal is to become a better man and make a better life for his family. He feels less than a man because other people provide for the children that he brought into this world.

Ean's textual description of his experience

Ean is a 29-year-old African American male who is the product of a single parent household. He has been arrested three times and incarcerated twice. His first arrest was at the age of 25. His drug of choice is marijuana. He did not graduate from high school, he is not married, and he has no children. Ean appeared ready to participate in the interview. The interview began with him sharing a little information about losing his father in early childhood and his initial experiences with drugs.

> My childhood was humbling. My mother slaved on her job just to make ends meet. We were a paycheck away from having nothing at all. If she lost her job, none of the bills would

be paid and we'd probably be living on the streets or have to move in with some of our family. I didn't have any siblings. I was spoiled. Throughout grade school I always handled my business because I understood how things were at home. I wasn't trouble, so I just tried to make ends meet. To help my mom out, cuz my dad passed away when I was four. I was 14 when I first tried drugs. My first experience was great. It made me chill out and relax. We were laughing and everything was kind of funny. I think it's just because my older cousin introduced me to it, I looked up to him. He told me he was going to get high for the first time, I saw him doing it and I just wanted to do it. I knew it won't the right thing to do, but if my cousin was doing it, it was cool. After the first time I wanted to keep getting high. Once I started getting high on a regular, school won't important. I would ditch school and meet my boys and spend the whole day just smoking weed. After a while I got so behind in school then I just stopped going. My mama begged me to go back, but I never did. It was hard for me to find work cuz I didn't have no education.... I started selling drugs to help my mama out. I hated it she had to slave at dead end jobs.

Ean's structural description of his experience

Ean wanted better for his mother; he wanted her to have a husband who would take care of her so that she did not have to work so hard. He resented the fact that his father was no longer there to care for the family. He vaguely remembers his father because he was so young when he passed. When he saw other children with their fathers, he wondered what their lives were like. His entire life consisted of struggling and living from paycheck to paycheck. Each time Ean went to prison it was because he was committing an illegal act in order to get money to feed his drug addiction. Since Ean's most recent release from prison he has been attempting to change his life and become drug-free. Upon his release from prison the last time, he was sent to a halfway house for a few months. He now rents a room until he can obtain steady employment. Ean is currently working odd jobs until he can get back on his feet.

He is on probation and meets with his probation officer every two weeks. Each time he has met with his probation officer since being released, he has passed his mandatory urinalysis. Ean revealed that as long as he does what is expected of him, he will never go back to prison. He stated that if he was afforded the opportunity to attend a residential drug rehabilitation program, he would take advantage of it. Ean realizes it is going to be very difficult for him to win his battle with drugs without professional help, but he is going to do everything in his power to remain drug-free.

Watching his mother struggle in order to feed him made him sad. He would visit his friends and their mothers would be home, helping with homework and preparing meals. His mother was the love of his life and the last thing he wanted to do was hurt her. He realizes now how much he hurt his mom when he quit school. At the time he did not see that all his mother wanted was for him to have a better life than she could provide for him. If he had it to do all over again, he would have never quit school.

Ean realizes now the importance of getting an education and staying out of trouble. He is considering going back to school, but it's hard being a felon. If only he knew then what he knows now. Ean asked if I could assist him with maybe getting back into school and into a drug rehabilitation center because going back to prison is not an option for him!

Jeremy's textual description of his experience

Jeremy is a 35-year-old African American male who has been the product of a single-parent as well as two-parent household. He has been arrested seven times and incarcerated two times. His first arrest was at the age of 18. He is married with two children, and his drug of choice is cocaine. Jeremy was a very pleasant young man and was quiet enthusiastic about sharing his story. He expressed vehemently at the beginning of the interview that he would never go back to prison. He began by describing the roles played by several significant adult family members in his childhood.

> My childhood was good. My uncle had a positive influence on my life. My father was never around. Me and my mom lived with my aunt and uncle until I was eight or nine. It was a lot of people in the house. I just think that my cousins were kind of abusive...everybody use to beat me if I did something wrong. My mom wasn't around a lot and I never had a relationship with my dad. I wouldn't even call him my dad. But I did feel loved as a child even from my mom who was always out partying. She had me when she was 17, she won't ready for no baby. She got a good job with the airlines when I was eight and we traveled to different places in the United States and a few other countries. She met her husband when I was ten, he was a good man. I resented him taking my mama away from me......so I started acting out, which led me to using drugs. They were great parents. I wanted to be a man. If I had a chance to do it all over again, I would have never touched drugs, which is why my life is so [explicit] up. Instead of me trying to be like them, I did everything I could to be bad. But

> I had the opportunity to have a good life and I blew it.

Jeremy's structural and textual description

Jeremy first experimented with drugs was when he was 13 years old. He was hanging out with friends, everyone was smoking marijuana, and he did not want to be the odd kid; therefore, he joined the crowd. He revealed that he was afraid after his first experience because he had to walk home by himself while he was high. He was afraid that his aunt or uncle would be home and realize that he was high and beat him. Once he arrived home and no one realized, he felt a great sense of relief. From that point on he became really good at hiding the fact that he was high from the adults at his house. His uncle traveled for work and was gone for days at a time, and his mother was not around a lot, which made it easier for him when he came home high.

> The first time I went to prison I was scared. I was scared cause I had to leave my wife and kids, umm… I was always the provider and now I had to worry if they were gonna be OK. I remember my mom dropped me off to turn myself in and my whole life flashed before my eyes…..I tried not to cry, but I couldn't help it. I had been so stupid and messed up my life. Now I had to do the time……. Once I got to

> prison it didn't take long to adjust. My wife lived a few hours away, she came to visit two times a month. I didn't want my kids to see me locked up...... we never told them I was in prison, they thought I was working cause I worked on the railroads and was gone a lot anyway. I would write and talk to them on the phone sometimes, my wife did a great job hiding it, but I missed my kids. My mama and uncle kept money on my books and I got lots of letters.....the time went faster than I thought. This last time I was locked up time went slow. I had no visitors for a year cause I was locked up 2500 miles from home. Just letters and phone calls. I learned to adjust to awww.... and didn't bother nobody and nobody bothered me. It was a bunch of rednecks, but I was cool with my homies.

Jeremy revealed that he was not offered drug rehabilitation at any point during his incarcerations. He stated that in order to receive drug rehabilitation, he had to have been sentenced to at least two years. He admitted to taking one or two drug classes, but nothing extensive that would help him with his addiction. Jeremy's second incarceration was due to violating his parole by failing a mandatory urinalysis test. He revealed that he was mandated to attend drug rehabilitation classes after failing two mandatory urinalysis tests. After his first release from prison,

Jeremy stated that he had employment waiting for him and was able to go right back to work. Since his last release, he has not been able to find steady employment, but he is doing odd jobs in order to provide for his family. He is currently home with his wife and children and vows that he will never go back to prison. Jeremy now attends Narcotics Anonymous classes at least once a week and has been clean for four months.

He recalls his life starting to change significantly when he started using drugs. At the age of 13 smoking marijuana gave him a sense of freedom. He could block out all of the bad feelings he held in about his abuse and his mother never being around. After the initial experience it was all downhill after that. Every time he got an opportunity he would get high. He was no longer afraid that the adults in his life would know that he was high, everybody was busy doing their own thing.

When he was 14 years old they moved to Philadelphia and little did he know, his life would forever change. He met other young boys his age who smoked marijuana and he fit right in. When he was 16 years old he was introduced to cocaine. He tried it and liked the feeling. He continued to do cocaine throughout his high school years. His use of cocaine caused major turmoil in his family. Jeremy stressed that he was defiant, disobedient, disrespectful and caused so much dysfunction in his home. At one point he was sent back to to live with his uncle and aunt. He respected his uncle, who was his idle.

Even thought he was under the iron fist of his uncle during his last year of high school, that did not stop him from getting high. He learned how to hide it and manipulate anyone who confronted him. Jeremy admitted that he is very good at manipulating anyone. He had several run-ins with the law after high school, but nothing major. He admitted that he was not afraid of anyone or anything because while using cocaine he felt invincible. He was using cocaine regularly while in high school, but it began to get out of control once he enrolled in college. It was so easy to obtain and he was good at manipulation. Being tall and handsome really helped manipulate the girls and being smart helped manipulate the guys.

Jeremy had his first real run in with the law while in college, but was bailed out by his mom and uncle. A year after that he was in trouble again and once again bailed out by his mom and uncle. Eventually he figured out that he could break the law in order to get drugs and would be bailed out. Well that worked for years, but eventually the crimes got more serious and he could not be bailed out. That is when the serious jail and prison time began. He often wonders if he had not been bailed out when he was younger, would his life be different.

Jeremy admits that his serious drug use has caused him to waste most of his life. He feels he is not the man that God put him on earth to be. He hopes he will live long enough to repair his life. He admits that he has an amazing wife who stands by him and shields his children from his drug and crime ridden life. He said there is not enough time left in a lifetime to repair all of the hurt and pain he has caused his wife and family. He stated he will spend every day of his life trying to repair his relationship with his wife and children.

He has the support of his family and has finally realized that he is too old to continuously live this life. He is trying to get into a drug rehabilitation program, but in the meantime he is staying away from the people, places and things that are triggers for his drug use. His only fear is that it is too late for him to change his life. Jeremy promises that after this probation period is over, he will never go back to prison again!!!!

Jeremy is a very intelligent young man with a college education. It was mind boggling listening to his interview. In my mind I was wondering how a young man who was so smart could make such poor life choices. While interviewing him he revealed that his life was not bad as a child, but he remembers having a problem with authority as early as six. He was very resentful when he was disciplined by anyone other than his mother and his uncle. He believes being disciplined so harshly by his cousins made him bitter as a young boy, which has a major impact on how he has dealt with life.

Purpose

The purpose of this study was to understand the lived experiences of non-violent African American males with a drug addiction who had recidivated. A small group of ten African American men were interviewed to gain an understanding of their lived experiences. Using a small sample allowed intimate descriptions from each participant and an in-depth interface between the participant and me. During each interview it was obvious that every participant had remorse for the lives they had ultimately chosen. Not one of the participants denied the fact they had bought shame not only on themselves, but their families and society as a whole.

It was apparent the participants with children wanted a better life for their children. They admitted their choice to use drugs had impacted their children's lives emotionally as well as financially. There were times during the interviews that some of the participants were in tears. Having to actually talk about their shortcomings and the effect it had on their loved ones was agonizing. It was as though it was the first time they actually realized they had negatively impacted so many other lives and not just their own. I asked each participant how they thought their decision to use drugs, which ultimately landed them behind bars had affected the entire African American race. Most said the obvious- there were more black men in prison than any other race, which left more black children without fathers, wives without husbands and mothers without sons. There were some discussions about the disparity between the number of blacks incarcerated compared to other races.

It was evident in each interview that the participants unequivocally accepted the responsibility of their choices. Each participant who did not have a father present in his life had a very strong opinion about their absence. It was evident that the participants put a lot of blame on their fathers for not being a positive influence in their lives. Most were not a constant figure in their children's lives; they looked at it differently than their fathers not being in their lives. The participants each accepted full responsibility for their choice to use drugs, but not one fully understood how their addiction was severely impacting their children's lives. Every participant expressed their children would be OK, because the mothers would protect the children, just as their mothers and grandmothers had tried to protect them.

Overview of the Interviews

While the participants described their lived experiences as African American males with addictions and had recidivated, it was quite apparent that the drug use at an early age and legal issues had a significant influence on their future choices and ultimately their lifestyles. Each participant spoke of very intimate and in depth experiences of their lives. Their lived experience provided the information needed for this book. Their shared experiences were: (a) being raised by a single parent, (b) drug use at an early age, (c) peer pressure, (d) family support during and after incarceration, (d) drug rehabilitation during and after incarceration, (e) employment after incarceration and (f) the effects incarceration has on their children.

Raised by a single parent

The majority of the participants spoke about their fathers not being present, either physically or mentally during the time they were growing up. Six of the ten participants were raised by their mother or grandmother. The absence of a father in the residence created a very tense as well as hectic home for the majority of the participants. Ideally, both parents should play a significant role in the lives of their children. Realistically, the majority of the participants' mothers experienced difficulty with their sons as teenagers because of their drug use at such early ages. A major trepidation for the mothers of the participants was being able to provide the basic necessities such as food, shelter and clothing. Each participant acknowledged that they were thankful for their mothers.

Parental absences are most frequent in highly disadvantaged communities that are comprised mainly of racial minorities. In the 20th century, W.E.B. DuBois (1899) expressed that urban black families are volatile due to slavery and economic hardship. In addition, approximately 72% of African American children are born out of wedlock. That does not necessarily mean their fathers are not in lives, it means their mothers and fathers are not married to each other. Research has indicated that children who do not have a father in the home usually receive less parental supervision, are more likely to engage in fights, and ultimately are more susceptible to criminal activity.

Early drug usage and peer pressure

Things that separate children from customary ideals and positivity can cause undesired emotions, which produce undesired behaviors. A customary objective for first time drug and alcohol use is peer pressure. Peer pressure is a significant aspect when it relates to teenagers experimenting with alcohol and drugs. The older teenagers get, the less influence peer pressure has on them. Although there have been political, federal, and educational programs to reduce drug usage in America, there has been an increase in drug intake among the nation's youth.

Early drug usage and peer pressure emerged for all but one of the ten participants, and he began using drugs at the age of 19 or 20. Of the nine participants who started using drugs during their teenage years, all decided to use because of peer pressure. The one participant revealed peer pressure was not the reason he first used drugs. His first experience was because the adults in his life were constantly badgering him not to do drugs, which made him want to experience it.

Family support during and after incarceration

Family support plays a substantial role in the life of a felon, ***before, during and after incarceration***. Families are key when it comes to ex-offenders becoming productive citizens of society and learning how to stay drug free in order to prevent recidivism. Many of the societal and structural concerns that criminals face after being set free from prison have been integrated into theories of persistence and desistence from offending (Laub & Sampson, 2003). Once ex-offenders are committed to making a change and acquire certain social bonds, they become attached to something or someone, such as family; they do not want to give up. Seven of the ten participants received tremendous financial and moral support from their family members while incarcerated and upon their release. Three participants did not receive support from their families because they did not have a strong relationship with their families before their incarceration.

Drug rehabilitation during and after incarceration

Recidivism rates are high for substance abuse offenders leaving prison and returning to the same communities. Research findings suggest that the recidivism rate is higher for prisoners who were not afforded the opportunity of any form of drug rehabilitation while incarcerated. The high recidivism rate is not only frightening for society, but for the African American race as a whole. It is essential for non-violent substance abusers to acquire some form of drug treatment, before, during, and after their imprisonment to prevent the high likelihood of recidivism. Of the ten participants who were interviewed, only one had received residential drug treatment after incarceration, and one had taken mandatory drug classes while incarcerated. The other eight participants expressed a desire to attend either drug rehabilitation and or Alcoholics Anonymous programs.

Theories

Much of the research regarding the incarceration of African American men focuses on four theories: financial strain, social control, labeling/stigma and social bonding/attachment. The financial strain theory suggests that children are at a large disadvantage when their fathers are incarcerated due to the loss of income. The loss of income in a family can directly affect a child's access to resources such as education and healthcare. One can assume that a number of fathers contributed to the family income before incarceration. Prisoners depend on support from the family while incarcerated, which further puts a strain on their families' income. Even when fathers are released, the financial woes do not cease. Unemployment can lead ex-offenders to resort to crime in order to feed their families or, in the case of an ex-offender with an addiction, to feed his addiction. This ultimately leads to the vicious cycle of recidivism.

The second theory is the social control theory, which implies that losing a father to incarceration could have emotional as well as behavioral effects on a child. It can diminish the quantity as well as quality of supervision that a child receives. The possibilities are higher for a child to misbehave or break rules when there is a lack of parental supervision. When fathers are imprisoned, there is usually not a strong male figure in the home. The third theory is social bonding theory, which is the sudden separation that occurs when a father goes to prison. The sudden separation can sometimes be emotionally traumatic for a child.

Participants with children

The families of the incarcerated drug offenders are affected by their stay in prison. It is important for offenders to maintain a relationship with their loved ones while incarcerated, especially their children. In most recent years, the number of African American males incarcerated has risen so quickly that it has become the norm for many families. It is estimated that 1 in 14 children have a parent who is incarcerated, and 94 percent of those parents are males. Incarceration plays a major role when the African American father is absent from the home. Research has indicated that children who do not have a father in the home usually receive less parental supervision, are more likely to engage in fights, and ultimately are more susceptible to criminal activity.

Children build up a trust with adults who care for them during the first two years of their lives. Having a father in prison can perhaps impede a child's progression of trust and can damage the possibility for future bonding with the father upon his release. Children who do visit are often disturbed by what they encounter. A prison is not an ideal place for a child to attempt to bond or build a relationship with his or her father.

Ultimately, some scholars suggest that labeling or the stigma of having a father in prison is reason for children to withdraw from their friends and even their own families. All of these theories only apply if the father was present in the lives of the children before incarceration. Many of the disadvantages related to children of incarcerated fathers may be due to the fact that the fathers are absent, but the potential incarceration may still cause a greater negative impact on a child's behavior. The stigma of imprisonment is not only linked to the prisoner himself, but also to those associated with him. When an individual goes to prison for committing a crime, violent or nonviolent, their loved ones, including their children, are connected with the socially unacceptable behavior.

It is not uncommon for a mother to refrain from telling her children that their father is incarcerated due to the shame that it brings them. In suburban neighborhoods, spouses and children who considered themselves upstanding citizens before the incarceration are often perceived and treated differently after the incarceration. For many low-income families from minority communities, having a father in prison is becoming customary; therefore, black children in these communities do not always experience the negative labeling as one may experience in middle class communities. The African American children in disadvantaged neighborhoods whose fathers are incarcerated are already more likely faced with emotional and behavioral problems because of where they live; to have a father in prison only compounds their difficulties in life.

Nevertheless, incarceration of any man places an enormous strain on a father-child relationship. The prison boom for the past 30 years has negatively impacted current generations. The shift has caused high jobless rates for low-skilled black men. Because of severe unemployment, many African

American men in disadvantaged communities commit non-violent crimes or sell drugs to make money. Since more disciplinary policies were put into place, the incarceration rate has multiplied by nearly 500 percent within the last 30 years, with the majority of the incarcerations directly impacting the African American community.

African American children whose fathers are incarcerated often find it difficult to maintain meaningful relationships. The imprisonment of the husband and father of the household places huge financial and emotional stresses on what may have already been a volatile situation caused by substance abuse. While incarcerated, the prisoner struggles to maintain some form of normal relationship with their children. Prisons are not designed to provide a pleasant or welcoming environment for families, especially children. If the families are fortunate enough to be within driving distance of the prison, they still have to endure a long wait in order to be able to see their loved one for one to two hours. The visit usually takes place in a large room that is otherwise used for another purpose on a normal day at the prison. The room is loud and crowded, and it provides no opportunity for any type of meaningful conversation.

For security reasons, it is very uncommon for a father to be able to have any form of interaction with their children during the visit. Although strong bonds between inmates and family members are signs of success after release, most prison systems do not encourage relationships between children and their inmate fathers because of the inhumane setting. Many fathers are in prisons that are located hours away from their loved ones, so family relationships are either absent or are mainly dysfunctional. Many of the fathers who are in prison, especially African American fathers, are not mentally prepared or equipped with the proper parental skills to raise or care for their children. When the convicted are released, there are certain reentry programs that are made available for them; unfortunately, the systems do not prepare the felons for the challenges of reuniting and parenting the children that were left behind.

A significant number of incarcerated fathers who have been found guilty of petty theft and drug offenses are likely to recidivate, especially those with substance abuse addictions. Sending the felons back to prison when they recidivate because of drug violations only exacerbates the already delicate relationships they have with their children. There are many ways in which the prison system can assist inmates who have children in order to strengthen the bond while the prisoner is away. Prison polices could be modified to allow for longer visits for prisoners with families as well as contact visits for nonviolent criminals.

There should be family-centered events scheduled during the holidays and special occasions. Fathers with young children should be given a chance to be involved in parenting programs. The parenting programs should continue upon their release. Community-based support systems would be a tremendous asset in assisting the prisoner and his children in rebuilding a supportive relationship once the prisoner is released.

Formative Years

The first five to six years of a child's life are the most important as far as building their emotional foundation. Their emotional foundation will become their emotional filter that he or she will use for the rest of their lives. As teenage moms, the majority are extremely naïve and inexperienced when they have their children. There is no exact science as to how a child will turn out, but their chances are impaired when they are reared in a single family home, by a teenage mother and a father who does not play an active role in their lives.

We, as parents, often think of psychological damage to a child as resulting from physical or sexual abuse, but that is not always the case. A child can be scared for life by the absence of a father or positive male role model in their lives. They can also be scared by the lack of nurturing from their mothers-either because the mother doesn't know better or just does not care. Whatever the case may be, we as mothers carry the most responsibility for these little black boys. It is our responsibility to do all that we can as mothers and that entails carefully choosing who we create lives with. What we as women should not want are little black boys growing up to be black men with a false start and headed straight to prison from the womb.

Summary of Results

All ten participants had abused illegal drugs and had been incarcerated on more than one occasion for committing non-violent crimes. Seven of the ten participants reported that their drug of choice was marijuana; two reported that it was cocaine, and one reported it was heroin. Three of the participants graduated from high school, two received GED's while incarcerated, four did not complete high school, and one completed three years of college. The average age at which the participants first used illicit drugs was 13.5 years. Five of the participants grew up in single-parent homes; two of those five lived in the home with their mother and grandparents. Four of the ten participants were raised by both parents, and one of the participants was raised by a single parent for five years before he turned 18 and went to college. Five of the ten participants are now employed, and five are not employed.

Inspiration to publish this book

A few years after doing the interviews, one day I received a phone call from one of the participants whom I had interviewed; he was back in prison.

He had violated parole because he did not pay child support. He explained that he could not pay child support because he could not find a job. He asked if I had finished the book that I was writing because he wanted to read it. I told him that I had not, but I would send him a copy of my dissertation. I explained to him that it was lengthy, but very interesting. After some research I realized that prisoners are not allowed to receive books from individuals, they had to be sent from book stores or publishing companies.

I then decided to turn my dissertation into a book, have it published and order him a copy from Amazon. Even though he was back in prison, he wanted to get it right. I was once told by a Corrections Officer that usually prisoners do not begin to realize how much of their lives they have wasted until they get older. When they are in and out of prison at a young age, they handle it better. When Father Time begins to creep up on them, that is when they realize how much of their lives have been wasted. This was the case with this prisoner. He said he was tired and did not have the energy to spend the rest of his life behind prison walls. He was only 30, but said he felt like he was an eighty-year-old man.

If reading a book will inspire him to make better choices, I will write as many books as needed. I will never give up on this population of young black men. I will never look down on them or judge them. I will spend the rest of my life trying to make a difference in their lives. If I only make a difference in one life, that's one less black man behind prison walls.

REFERENCES

Aubry, L. (2010). African American prison rates soaring; What else is new? *Sentinel.*

Austin, J., & Hardyman, P. L. (2004). The risk and needs of the returning prisoner population. *The Review of Policy Research, 2,* 1.

Baron, S. W. (2007). Street youth, gender, financial strain, and crime: Exploring Broidy and Agnew's extension to general strain theory. *Deviant Behavior, 28,* 3.

Doi: 10.1080/01639620701233217. Retrieved from: http:www.tandfonline.com/doi/abs/10.1080/01639620701233217.

Brame, R., Bushway, S. D., & Paternoster, R. (2003). Examining the prevalence of criminal desistance. *Criminology, 41,* 432-488.

Dubois, WEB (1903). The Souls of Black Folk. New York, Bantam Classic

Dyer, W. J. (2005). Prisons, fathers and identity: a theory of how incarceration affects men's paternal identity, *Fathering, 3*(3), 201.

Guerino, P. M., Harrison, P., & Sabol, W. J. (2011). *Prisoners in 2010*. Retrieved from http://www.ncjrs.gov/App/Publications/abstract.aspx?ID=258085

Hirschi, T. & Gottfredson, M. R. (1993). Commentary: Testing the general theory of crime. *Journal of Research in Crime and Delinquency. 30*(1), 47-54. Retrieved from http:www.criminology.fsu.edu/crimtheory/hirschi.htm.

Johnson, S.L., (2006). Choosing recovery from substance abuse and dependence: *The Journey* of *Understanding*. Alliant International University: Fresno, CA.

Jones, M. (2004). Maslow's hierarchy of needs can lower recidivism. *Corrections Today, 7,* 18-22.

Laub, J. H., & Sampson, R. J. (2003). Shared Beginnings, Divergent Lives: Delinquent

Boys to Age 70. Cambridge, MA: Harvard University Press.

Princeton University (2004), *The fragile families and child well-being study*. Retrieved from: http://crcw.princetonedu/fragilefamilies.

Reed, W. (2010). *Recidivism among Black Americans*. Blauvelt, NY: Hudson Valley Press.

CPSIA information can be obtained at www.ICGtesting.com
Printed in the USA
BVOW02s1940270916

463474BV00006B/13/P